TIME FOR KIDS READERS

Visit the Capitol

by Lisa Trumbauer

Harcourt

Orlando Austin Chicago New York Toronto London San Diego

Visit *The Learning Site!*
www.harcourtschool.com

This is the United States Capitol. It is in Washington, D.C.

The United States Congress works here. The Congress is the part of the government that makes laws.

This part of the building is called the north wing. The Senate lawmakers work here.

This is the south wing. The House of Representatives lawmakers work here.

This is the dome. It
is made of iron.

This is the Statue of Freedom.
It sits on top of the dome.

This is the rotunda. It is the round room inside the dome.